NEW VANGUARD 292

ITALIAN DESTROYERS OF WORLD WAR II

MARK STILLE   ILLUSTRATED BY PAUL WRIGHT

OSPREY PUBLISHING

Bloomsbury Publishing Plc

Kemp House, Chawley Park, Cumnor Hill, Oxford OX2 9PH, UK

29 Earlsfort Terrace, Dublin 2, Ireland

1385 Broadway, 5th Floor, New York, NY 10018, USA

E-mail: info@ospreypublishing.com

www.ospreypublishing.com

OSPREY is a trademark of Osprey Publishing Ltd

First published in Great Britain in 2021

© Osprey Publishing Ltd, 2021

A catalog record for this book is available from the British Library.

ISBN: PB 9781472840554; eBook 9781472840561
ePDF 9781472840530; XML 9781472840547

21 22 23 24 25   10 9 8 7 6 5 4 3 2 1

Index by Zoe Ross
Typeset by PDQ Digital Media Solutions, Bungay, UK
Printed and bound in India by Replika Press Private Ltd.

Osprey Publishing supports the Woodland Trust, the UK's leading woodland conservation charity.

To find out more about our authors and books visit **www.ospreypublishing.com**. Here you will find extracts, author interviews, details of forthcoming events and the option to sign up for our newsletter.

Acknowledgements

The author would like to thank Maurizio Brescia for his immense assistance, particularly in providing the photographs for this book.

Explanation of RM Destroyer Names

Mirabello class – Italian admirals of the late 19th century

Leone class – big cats: Lion, Panther, and Tiger

Sella class – Italian statesmen of the late 19th century

Sauro class – Italian patriots who were killed during the *Risorgimento* or the First World War

Turbine class – wind phenomena

Navigatori class – Italian explorers of the 13th, 14th, and 15th century

Freccia class – Italian words for arrow or dart

Folgore class – synonyms for lightning

Maestrale class – winds from the intermediate quadrants of the compass

Oriani class – poets and scholars of the 19th century

Soldati class – soldiers belonging to corps or specialized units of the Italian armed forces

Comandanti class – commanding officers killed in action and given Italy's highest military decoration (the *Medaglia d'Oro al Valor Militaire*)

Title page image

All three surviving second-series Soldati-class ships were handed over to the French as war reparations in 1948. Here *Mitragliere* is shown in Taranto in her postwar configuration and colors in 1947. Note the ship has received the amidships 4.7in gun. *Mitragliere* was handed over on July 15, 1948, renamed *Jurien de la Gravière*, and was stricken by the French Navy in 1956 after no operational service. (M. Brescia Collection)

CONTENTS

ITALIAN DESTROYERS OF WORLD WAR II

INTRODUCTION

The Italian Royal Navy (*Regia Marina* or RM) operated one of the largest destroyer fleets of World War II. At the start of the war, the RM deployed 59 destroyers. It built another five during the war and captured and placed into service a similar number of foreign destroyers. The RM fought a prolonged and costly naval campaign which accounted for 50 of the 59 pre-war destroyers. RM destroyers fought not only in the Mediterranean, but also in a forgotten campaign in the Red Sea.

The RM's mission at the start of the war was to keep the sea lines of communications open to North Africa and Albania and deny the Strait of Sicily and Central Mediterranean to the British. The Italians planned to use their battle fleet to underpin their control of the Central Mediterranean, but calculated that any large battle fought to a conclusion would be costly. The RM had no prospect of replacing large ships lost during the war, so there was a universal reluctance among naval commanders, and often direct orders from higher command, not to risk the fleet against a superior enemy force. RM on-scene commanders were continually handicapped by restrictive orders that forbade engagement unless a clear superiority was evident.

Tactically, the RM was very conservative due to restrictive rules of engagement from naval headquarters and a doctrine of fighting battles at long range. This translated into a very defensive posture for the escorting destroyers, which seldom had the opportunity to employ their guns at effective ranges or to make aggressive torpedo attacks. Because of a defect in RM naval gunnery, shared by its destroyers, the RM had no success with its doctrine of long-range gunnery actions. The main weapon of Italian destroyers was a heavy main gun battery, not their torpedoes. On the few occasions during the war when Italian destroyers were called on to conduct torpedo attacks, their small torpedo battery proved to be a disadvantage.

RM destroyers were also handicapped by a variety of technical factors. They carried inferior guns and poor torpedo fire control systems. Very few carried radar and those that did only did so for a short period before the Italian surrender in

The RM's destroyers, like those destroyers in any navy, were the workhorses of the fleet. They were present in all fleet actions in the Mediterranean and were the mainstays for convoy escort. This is a view of Navigatori-class ship *Da Verazzano* in 1941 taken as the destroyer steams at high speed. (M. Brescia Collection)

Gioberti seen leaving Cagliari in late summer 1942. The destroyer built a fine war record fighting at Calabria, Matapan, First and Second Sirte, and the operations to supply Axis forces in Tunisia in early 1943. *Gioberti* was finally sunk in August 1943 by British submarine *Simoom* on August 9, 1943 off La Spezia. (M. Brescia Collection)

September 1943. As antisubmarine warfare (ASW) platforms, RM destroyers were largely ineffective because of a lack of sensors and weapons. Endurance was also an issue, even in the closed waters of the Mediterranean. Finally, seaworthiness was a major design problem of most destroyers built before the Maestrale class was commissioned in the mid-1930s. In general, it is fair to say that the RM's destroyer force underperformed and did not have a great impact on the naval war in the Mediterranean.

RM DESTROYER DESIGN AND DEVELOPMENT

When the Italians entered World War I in 1915, the RM had a fleet of 33 destroyers with another 16 under construction. In addition, there were some 85 small torpedo boats in service. The main operating area for the RM was

The three ships of the Leone class, including the *Pantera* shown here in 1935, were obsolescent by the start of the war. In 1939, they were deployed to the Italian colony of Eritrea, indicating that the RM considered them expendable if war came with the United Kingdom. The three ships fought a sporadic campaign in the Red Sea against the British until April 1941 when all three ships were scuttled. (M. Brescia Collection)

the Adriatic Sea where it was tasked to bottle up the Austro-Hungarian Navy. In this endeavor, the RM was largely successful, but Austro-Hungarian and German U-boats were able to ravage shipping in the Mediterranean from bases in the Adriatic for almost the entire war. At the conclusion of the war, the RM received seven Austro-Hungarian and three German destroyers, but these were all out of service by 1939 and thus saw no action in World War II.

Since RM destroyers were required to operate only in the nearby waters of the Adriatic and later the Mediterranean, they were not designed with endurance in mind or built as heavily as British destroyers, which had to be suitable for operations all over the world. The light scale of construction produced fast ships, which was a traditional RM design priority. Feeding this penchant for speed was the Italian practice of paying shipyards extra if the ships exceeded their design speed. This was often accomplished by running trials with no weapons fitted to produce the desired high speeds. Unfortunately for the RM, these high trial speeds had little bearing on the speeds achieved in operational service. RM destroyer designers also emphasized a heavy gun armament and soon settled on the 4.7in weapon as the standard main battery gun. Torpedo fits on RM destroyers were on the light side and ASW weaponry virtually non-existent. The capability to carry mines was important to the RM and was included in all destroyer classes.

During World War I, the RM had little opportunity to produce new ships, but moved from building scout cruisers (*esploratori*) in favor of large destroyers (*esploratori leggeri* or light scouts). The first of the large destroyers were the three ships of the 1,750-ton Mirabello class, which were well-armed and had a top speed of 35kt. The next class of large destroyers, the Leone class, was even more powerfully armed with four dual 4.7in mounts and displaced 2,200 tons. These were ordered in 1917, but they were not started until 1921 because of a shortage of steel and other materials. The Leone-class ships were more light cruiser than destroyer, and the next three classes of

Lanzerotto Malocello shown a few days before her launch at Genoa on March 14, 1929. The 12 ships of the Navigatori class were designed as counters to large French destroyers already in service. (M. Brescia Collection)

16 total ships commissioned between 1926 and 1928 reverted to a smaller hull. Armament was reduced, but the high speed was retained. All of these ships possessed stability problems, and their endurance was unsatisfactory, even for Mediterranean operations.

The focus of RM wartime planning shifted to France after World War I. Neither France nor Italy was in an economic condition to start any large naval construction program after the war, but each navy kept a wary eye on the other and designed warships to gain an advantage over its potential enemy. Competition with France led directly to the resumption of large destroyer construction by the RM. These were the 12 ships of the Navigatori class built between 1927 and 1931 to counter the 12 large French destroyers built between 1922 and 1931. These ships mounted a heavy main battery of six 4.7in guns in three twin mounts and possessed a design speed up to 38kt.

Although the Navigatori were the RM's last large destroyers, the size of subsequent classes continued to grow as Italian designers sought to create ships with the standard armament of two twin 4.7in mounts and two triple 21in torpedo mounts, combined with a high speed and acceptable seaworthiness. This balance was finally achieved in the four-ship Maestrale class completed in 1934. These ships also rectified the unreliability issues with Italian destroyer machinery. Prior to the Italian entry into the war in June 1940, the RM completed another 16 ships of a very similar design. The same design was used for wartime construction of destroyers, which amounted to a paltry five ships.

RM destroyer weapons

Italian destroyers were designed primarily as gun platforms. Unfortunately for the RM, their naval gunnery was generally ineffective. The standard 4.7in gun was a good weapon, but the design of its mount was flawed and created excessive salvo dispersion. The tighter the salvo, the better the possibility of scoring a hit once the target had been bracketed. Salvo dispersion was caused by the twin 4.7in guns being mounted on a single cradle. The guns were placed too close together, which caused the shells to interfere with each

The standard main battery weapon aboard almost all RM destroyers was the twin 4.7in mount. This weapon was produced by different manufacturers and had various modifications, but all had the guns placed in a single cradle, as shown here in this view of the amidships 4.7in mount aboard a Navigatori-class destroyer. The two gun barrels were spaced only inches apart which meant when they fired, the shells interfered with each other. The resulting dispersion made accurate gunnery virtually impossible. (M. Brescia Collection)

other in flight. Another problem contributing to salvo dispersion was the excessive muzzle velocity of Italian guns. The RM accepted this to get longer ranges but, combined with inconsistent powder charge performance, the result was salvo dispersion.

Italian fire control systems were well-designed and comparable to those of other navies of the period. These fire control systems were derived from British Barr & Stroud devices provided in the early 1920s. Two Italian firms, San Giorgio and Officine Galileo, produced fire control equipment for the RM. By the 1930s, the RM had developed two fire control systems, one designed for destroyers. This system remained in service throughout the war. It was simple to operate and needed four to five operators. The Navigatori class introduced the standard arrangement for RM destroyer fire control systems. A heavy fire control director sat atop the bridge with the mechanical computer below the navigation bridge in a protected space. Two 9ft 10in rangefinders were also located atop the bridge. Abaft the after funnel was a second fire control director. The aft fire control director was found to be useless under operational conditions, and to reduce top weight, it was removed from RM destroyers.

The 4in guns on RM early destroyers were based on British designs produced under license by Ansaldo. They were produced in a single-gun version and in an M1919 version with a twin mounting in a common cradle.

The RM standard destroyer main battery gun was a 4.7in gun. A new 50-caliber version from 1926 was introduced on the Navigatori class. It fired a projectile weighing almost 52lb. At an elevation of 45 degrees, its maximum range was 21,430yd. Unfortunately for the RM, the standard twin mount placed the guns close together in a common cradle. The initial muzzle velocity of 3,117ft/sec was reduced to 3,018ft/sec, but this failed to correct the dispersion problem.

RM destroyer antiaircraft capabilities were inadequate. From the mid-1930s, RM antiaircraft doctrine was to employ barrage fire. The scale of the air threat to RM destroyers was not heavy early in World War II, but destroyers escorting convoys were exposed to torpedo bomber attacks from British aircraft based on Malta. Against torpedo bombers, which had to fly a straight course, RM antiaircraft doctrine and the few short-range antiaircraft guns aboard destroyers were effective. However, the RM's weak antiaircraft capabilities were not fully exposed until early 1943 when destroyers were subjected to heavy air attack while escorting convoys to Tunisia. The main battery guns on RM destroyers were not dual purpose, so they were worthless for antiaircraft work, which meant these ships lacked a long-range antiaircraft weapon. The only intermediate-range antiaircraft weapon on destroyers was the single 40mm gun dating from 1917 built under license from Vickers. There was only one 40mm on the beam of each destroyer and it was optically guided. At the start of the war the weak 40mm battery was augmented by 13.2mm machine guns, which were also optically guided. These fired a small shell and didn't have the range of the enemy guns.

The RM deployed better antiaircraft weapons on its destroyers as the war progressed, but these did not have fire control systems and were deployed in insufficient numbers. The best weapon was the 37mm/54 Breda gun fitted on destroyers in single mounts. This weapon was developed in 1930, proved reliable in service, but it was fed by a six-round magazine which reduced the rate of fire. Some destroyers were fitted with two of these.

The 40mm and 13.2mm guns were replaced by the 20mm/65 gun, which was fitted aboard destroyers in twin and single versions. This weapon was very reliable, but its effective range was assessed by the Italians to be only about 1,300yd.

Italian destroyers deployed smokescreens in defense of the convoys. The Royal Air Force (RAF) used low-level profiles to attack surface ships, which meant that even the 20mm and 13.2mm guns on RM destroyers were effective. RAF losses to antiaircraft fire during convoy attacks were often heavy, but so were losses to Axis shipping.

RM destroyer weapons

Type	Shell weight (lb)	Muzzle velocity (ft/sec)	Max range (yd)	Rate of fire (rounds per minute)
4.7in/45	51	2,789	16,950	5–6
4.7in/50	51.8	3,117	21,430	5–6
4.7in/15 illumination howitzer	43.7	1,312	7,000	5–6
4in/45 Schneider-Canet 1917	30.3	2,789	16,400	Up to 8
40mm/39 Vickers-Terni 1917	2	2,000	4,900	50-round ammunition boxes
37mm/54 Breda 1932	1.8	2,625	8,530	140
20mm/65 Breda 1935	.3	2,756	6,000	240
13.2mm/75.7 Breda M1931	1.8 ounce	2,592	6,600	500

In comparison to destroyers from other navies, Italian destroyers carried a light torpedo battery. The standard 21in RM destroyer torpedo (usually fitted in two triple mounts) possessed a mediocre range of 4,400yd at 46kt to 13,100yd at 29kt. These weapons were fitted with a 595lb warhead and proved reliable in service. Though the torpedo itself was a decent weapon, its fire control system was poor. RM destroyer doctrine in a fleet engagement was to keep at least one-third of the available torpedoes in reserve in the expectation that other torpedo opportunities would be available in a single engagement.

RM destroyers were not designed, equipped or trained to conduct ASW. Before the war, RM destroyers did not carry sonar. The few Italian-made sonars that became available during the war, and the few devices provided by the Germans, were usually fitted on ships designed and employed for ASW – the RM's torpedo boats and destroyer escorts. Only 12 destroyers were fitted with sonar by June 1942. Thus, for most RM destroyers, the only way to detect an enemy submarine was by spotting it on the surface, or much more unlikely, spotting its periscope. The most common method of detection was by observing a torpedo fired by the submarine and tracing it back to where the submarine fired from. By the time the destroyer arrived at the point of origin this made a successful depth charge attack a matter of luck. During the war, RM destroyers carried a limited number of depth charges which were rolled off the stern. Late in the war, some destroyers received depth-charge projectors, which could throw a projectile up to 120yd from the ship. A variety of depth charges were available, which had hydrostatic fuses that could be set for depths down to 328ft.

RM destroyer radar

One of the RM's principal weaknesses was the lack of radar aboard its surface ships. This placed the RM's destroyers at a severe disadvantage, especially in night combat, since the British deployed radar on surface ships early in the war and because they actively sought night engagements. The Italian electronics industry was unable to develop a reliable radar, so the RM asked the German Navy for assistance. The Fu.Mo 21/39 "De Te" radar was provided in small numbers and fitted on only three destroyers. The first Italian-produced radar was the EC.3 "Gufo" (Owl). Only 12 of these were delivered before Italy's surrender in September 1943. This radar was capable of surface and air search, but it was not accurate enough to permit radar-controlled gunnery. The EC.3/ter was the production version. Its theoretical maximum range, subject to many operational and atmospheric

Navigatori-class destroyers *Pigafetta* (left) and *Pancaldo* seen at Gaeta in April 1943. Both ships received wartime modifications; visible among these is the addition of single 20mm mounts on the quarterdeck of both ships. *Pancaldo* had her aft torpedo mount removed in favor of two 37mm/54 single mounts. Note the EC.3/ter radar atop *Pancaldo's* bridge. Only eight RM destroyers received any form of radar during the war. (M. Brescia Collection)

A

THE EARLY DESTROYERS

1 This is Mirabello-class destroyer *Riboty* in her 1942 configuration. Note the ship retains only four 4in single mounts and her torpedo mounts have been removed.

2 This is a 1942 view of *Sella*. The ship retains her pre-war configuration with a twin 4.7in mount fore and aft, two twin torpedo mounts, two 40mm single mounts and two 13.2 machine guns on the bridge.

3 This is *Turbine* in her 1942 configuration. The Turbine class was the final development of the series begun with the Sella class. *Turbine* has a heavier bridge structure and a platform between the torpedo mounts, which originally provided space for the second fire control director, but by 1942 it had been removed and replaced by 20mm antiaircraft guns. Note the camouflage scheme features white on the bow and stern, as well as the Taranto variant of curved lines for the dark gray pattern.

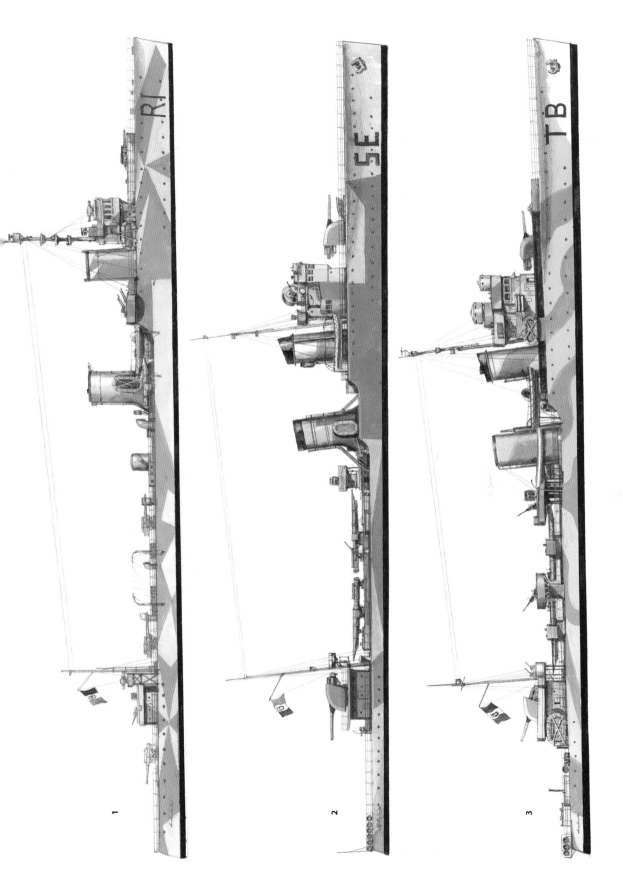

1

2

3

conditions, was approximately 16nm against a large surface target and up to 50 miles against aerial targets. This set was fitted on five destroyers.

RM DESTROYERS AT WAR

The RM began the war with 59 destroyers. The great majority was assigned to the two main squadrons; the First Squadron centered around the battleships and the Second Squadron centered around the heavy cruisers. Destroyers were organized into flotillas (*squadriglia cacciatorpediniere*) usually composed of four ships of the same class.

Italy entered the war on June 10, 1940. The immediate task of the RM was to supply Italian forces in North Africa. RM destroyers played a major role in this endeavor, acting as convoy escorts or as fast transports. The first naval clash of the war came on June 28 when the Royal Navy (RN) detected the 2nd Destroyer Flotilla (composed of *Espero*, *Ostro* and *Zeffiro*) west of Crete headed for Tobruk with high-priority military cargo. The RN planned an intercept with an overwhelming force of five light cruisers. The cruisers spotted the Italian force before dusk and opened fire at long range. *Espero* was limited to 25kt by a machinery defect, so the Italian commander ordered the destroyer, with him aboard, to engage the British while the other two ships escaped. *Espero* fought bravely, launching three torpedoes and hitting one of the cruisers with a 4.7in shell, but was overwhelmed by 6in gunfire. The destroyer sank with the loss of all but 53 of the 225 crewmen.

The Battle of Calabria

The first major encounter between the RM and the British Mediterranean Fleet occurred in July. Both the First and Second Squadrons were present with a total of 16 destroyers directly involved in the engagement. In the action fought on the afternoon of July 9, the RM employed its doctrine of fighting at long range. After some 40 minutes of long-range gunnery, one of the Italian battleships was hit by a British 15in shell and appeared to be heavily damaged. In accordance with his orders, the Italian commander decided to break off the action. He ordered his destroyers to cover the withdrawal. For the only time in the war, RM destroyers made large-scale torpedo attacks in a fleet action. Five attacks were made; the first was with five torpedoes from 13,500yd, the second with 10 torpedoes from 8,500yd, and the third with 10 more torpedoes from 11,000 to 13,800yd. None of the torpedoes found a target. The next attack with four more torpedoes also missed and the final attack with three torpedoes was also ineffective. In addition, the Italian

B **TARIGO IN ACTION**
On April 16, 1941, Folgore-class destroyers *Lampo* and *Baleno* and Navigatori-class destroyer *Tarigo* were escorting a five-ship convoy when it was attacked by four large British Tribal-class destroyers. The British encountered *Baleno* first and soon left her a burning hulk. All of the transports were then shot up or torpedoed and all were lost. *Tarigo* raced to engage the British ships. At close range, two of the British destroyers targeted *Tarigo*, killing the ship's captain and all other officers except one ensign. He took command, and with his ship on fire and sinking, ordered two torpedoes should be fired at a nearby British destroyer. Both struck *Mohawk*, which led to her loss. *Tarigo* also sank, but the torpedoing of *Mohawk* was the most successful Italian destroyer action of the entire war.

The first Soldati-class destroyer sunk during the war was *Artigliere*. Four Soldati-class ships of the 11th Destroyer Flotilla encountered British light cruiser *Ajax* in the early hours of October 12, 1940 off Cape Passero. The destroyers were engaged in turn by *Ajax* and two of the destroyers were damaged by 6in gunfire. *Artigliere* fought back gamely, firing a torpedo that missed, but then hit *Ajax* with four 4.7in shells at close range, which killed 13 and wounded 22 on the cruiser. Damage to *Artigliere* was severe, but the crew put out the fires and got one boiler working so the ship could head back to port. *Camicia Nera* later took *Artigliere* under tow, but three British cruisers arrived on the scene after dawn. The tow was dropped, and heavy cruiser *York* finished off the destroyer with two torpedoes after 8in gunfire failed to do the job. This view shows *Artigliere*'s final moments. (M. Brescia Collection)

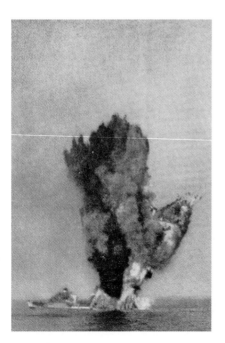

destroyers fired hundreds of 4.7in rounds with no results. Despite this, the torpedo attacks and the heavy smoke laid by the destroyers allowed the Italian fleet to break contact. None of the Italian destroyers were damaged. The Battle of Calabria, the largest naval engagement in the Mediterranean during the war, ended indecisively with no ships sunk on either side.

The Italians were not afraid to fight. On August 31, the RM's entire battle fleet, including 39 destroyers, sortied to engage a British convoy headed for Malta. No contact was made, and the Italian commander followed his restrictive orders and returned to port. Additional battle fleet operations were mounted September 7 to 9 and September 29 to October 1, but again made no contact with the British. Interspersed with major fleet operations, Italian destroyers fought a series of smaller actions as part of convoy escort operations or during attempts to attack British convoys headed to Malta. One of these actions occurred off Cape Passero on October 12. A single British light cruiser engaged four destroyers of the 11th Destroyer Flotilla and three torpedo boats. The action occurred at night and the confused Italians could never bring their superior numbers to bear. Cruiser *Ajax* sank two of the torpedo boats with 6in gunfire before the destroyers could engage. Destroyer *Geniere* took two 6in shell hits and lost contact. *Artigliere* suffered greater damage, but managed to hit the cruiser with four 4.7in rounds at close range killing 13 crewmen. The destroyer was taken in tow by *Camicia Nera*, but when three more British cruisers were spotted in the morning, the tow was abandoned. Heavy cruiser *York* dispatched the damaged *Artigliere*.

The Battle of Cape Spartivento (Battle of Cape Teulada to the RM)

Following the British attack on the RM's battle fleet in Taranto on the night of November 11/12 when carrier aircraft took three Italian battleships out of action, the RM sortied its battle fleet just two weeks later to intercept a British convoy headed for Malta. The Italian force consisted of two battleships, five heavy cruisers, and 14 supporting destroyers. Facing them was a British force with one battleship, one battlecruiser, five cruisers (one heavy), and ten destroyers. The resulting Battle of Cape Spartivento began on November 27 with an hour-long long-range gunnery duel from between 16,000 and 23,000yd. The Italian destroyers played a defensive role, but *Lanciere* was targeted by a light cruiser and hit by three 6in shells. The destroyer lost power, but was eventually towed back to port after the British chose not to pursue.

Debacle at Matapan

In 1941, the Germans entered the war in the Mediterranean. One of the results was that they pressed the RM to be more aggressive. In response, the Italians planned a major operation into the Eastern Mediterranean. Assigned to conduct this complex operation was a force of one battleship, six heavy cruisers, two light cruisers, and 17 destroyers. The Italians departed on March 26 to conduct their planned sweeps of the Aegean Sea and off the southwestern coast of Crete. By the next day, it was apparent that the Italians had lost the all-important element of surprise, but the operation was not canceled. Unbeknown to the RM, the British were at sea in strength. A cruiser duel during the morning of March 28 off Gaudo Island south of Crete was indecisive. Following a British carrier air attack, which inflicted no damage, the Italian commander decided to return home. The battle looked to be over, but continual British air attacks damaged the Italian battleship, which was able to escape, but also hit a heavy cruiser with a torpedo and brought her to a stop.

The Italian commander had no idea that the bulk of the RN's Mediterranean Fleet was nearby, so he sent two more cruisers supported by the 9th Destroyer Flotilla to tow the damaged cruiser home. At 2210 hours, radar aboard one of the British battleships gained contact on the crippled Italian cruiser and the other ships coming to her aid. The British reacted quickly and hit the two assisting cruisers with 15in shells before they could return fire. The destroyers were also surprised. *Alfieri* and *Carducci* were

Minelaying was an important design consideration for Italian destroyers and an important wartime mission. Almost every RM destroyer was fitted with mine rails with the mines being deployed over the stern. Here, Navigatori-class destroyers *Pessagno* and *Pigafetta* are shown laying mines in the Strait of Sicily on July 7, 1941. (M. Brescia Collection)

hit by 6in and 4.7in shells and later sank. *Oriani* attempted a counterattack with torpedoes, but was hit by a 4.7in shell and was forced to retire. Only *Gioberti* escaped undamaged.

Convoy battles

In April 1941, the RN deployed a squadron of four destroyers to Malta with the intent of attacking Axis convoys to North Africa. On the night of April 16 near the Kerkennah Bank off northern Tunisia, this unit intercepted a convoy of five merchant ships escorted by destroyers *Tarigo*, *Baleno*, and *Lampo*. The British destroyers did not use their radar, but still gained an advantage. In a brilliant action, the British sank all five merchants and *Baleno* and *Tarigo*. In return, a torpedo from *Tarigo* sank destroyer *Mohawk*. The last Italian destroyer, *Lampo*, was slow to get into action and was badly damaged by gunfire. She grounded on Kerkennah Bank to keep from sinking and was later salvaged, returning to service in 1942 after extensive repairs.

Despite this disaster, the RM's focus on the convoy battle was largely successful during the first half of 1941. From January to June 1941, 94 percent of Axis cargoes arrived safely. For several reasons, this dropped to 73 percent for the second half of 1941. One reason was the return of RN surface forces to Malta when two cruisers and two destroyers (designated Force K) arrived on October 21. Force K was vectored onto an Italian convoy on the night of November 9. The RM had allocated a strong escort of six destroyers to the seven-ship convoy. Another two heavy cruisers and four destroyers provided close support. Using radar, Force K avoided action with the covering force and proceeded to shoot up the entire convoy. The efforts of the Italian destroyers to protect the convoy were fruitless; *Fulmine* was hit by a barrage of shells and sank within minutes. *Grecale*, *Euro*, and *Maestrale* were all damaged. The British exchanged fire with the two Italian cruisers after destroying the convoy. The battle demonstrated the RM's total failure to prepare for night action, highlighted the importance of radar, and exemplified the effect of poor leadership. Force K savaged another convoy on November 24 escorted by RM torpedo boats, and again on December 1 when it sank destroyer *Alvise Da Mosto* and the single merchant ship she was escorting.

Without exception, RM destroyers came off second best in night actions against the British. One of these occasions was on April 16, 1941 when three Italian destroyers escorting a five-ship convoy were attacked by four British destroyers. The British achieved surprise, even without using radar, and sank two destroyers, one by gunfire and one by torpedo, and then dispatched all five of the merchants – the small German transports *Adana*, *Arta*, *Aegina*, *Iserlhon* and the Italian *Sabaudia*. The last Italian destroyer, *Lampo*, was slow to react and in a duel with destroyer *Nubian* was badly damaged. She was grounded on the Kerkennah Bank to keep from sinking. This is *Lampo* in late April 1941 after being towed to port for repairs. (M. Brescia Collection)

Libeccio was one of the escort ships of the seven-ship "Duisburg" convoy that was attacked by Force K on the night of November 9. Despite a very heavy escort of six destroyers, another two heavy cruisers, and four destroyers providing close support, a British force of two light cruisers and two destroyers annihilated the entire convoy and sank a destroyer of the escort while damaging three more. This was one of the most humiliating defeats of the RM during the war. *Libeccio* survived the battle, but the next morning was torpedoed by British submarine *Upholder* east of Sicily. The destroyer was taken in tow by *Euro*, but flooding caused her to sink, as shown here. Only one Italian destroyer survived after being torpedoed, but several survived mine damage. (M. Brescia Collection)

First and Second Battles of Sirte

Axis naval fortunes rebounded in late 1941 to early 1942. Convoy movements by both sides into the central Mediterranean led to two major clashes known as the First and Second Battles of Sirte. The first action occurred in December 1941 when the RM mounted a major convoy operation to North Africa at the same time as the British were moving a convoy to Malta. On December 17, an RM force of three battleships, two heavy cruisers, and ten destroyers engaged the British force covering the convoy, which consisted of four light cruisers and 12 destroyers. The late-afternoon gunnery duel was indecisive with only a single British destroyer being damaged. Two days later, a British force of three cruisers and four destroyers from Malta ran into a minefield off Tripoli, while trying to attack the Italian convoy. The minefield, laid by RM light cruisers and destroyers, sank one cruiser and a destroyer, and another cruiser was damaged. The large Italian convoy arrived safely, which allowed the Axis to consider the First Battle of Sirte a victory.

The RN mounted another major operation in March to get a convoy through to Malta. The action fought on March 22 was known as the Second Battle of Sirte. An RM force of one battleship, two heavy cruisers, one light cruiser, and seven destroyers was dispatched to intercept the convoy. In a day action fought in extremely rough seas and at long range, the RM damaged six British ships in exchange for only a single 4.7in hit on the battleship. The Italian destroyers were used to screen the heavy ships. The RM could claim victory when the British convoy was forced to change course to the south instead of proceeding directly to Malta as planned. This allowed German aircraft to sink one of the four merchant ships at sea and the other three in harbor.

Italian convoys proceeded to Libya largely unimpeded in April and May. In June, the British attempted to get another convoy through to Malta. The RM dispatched its battle fleet from Taranto on June 14 to stop it. The force of two battleships, two heavy cruisers, two light cruisers, and 12 destroyers was much more powerful than the convoy's escort. Against this superior force, the British abandoned the attempt on June 15. Concurrently, another British convoy approached Malta from the west. The RM could only muster two light cruisers and five destroyers to attack this convoy. In the ensuing engagement on the morning of June 15, the Italians battled the convoy escort of one light cruiser, five destroyers, and four destroyer escorts.

The action opened with a long-range gunnery duel between the two Italian cruisers and the five British destroyers. The Italian destroyers also engaged the British with their main batteries, but without success. Early in the battle, destroyers *Vivaldi* and *Malocello* got within 6,300yd of the convoy and fired four torpedoes without success. As the action continued, the British destroyer escorts placed a shell in *Vivaldi*'s forward boiler room and brought her to a halt. The destroyer eventually got one turbine operational, and she survived the fight. Two of the convoy's five merchant ships were damaged by air attacks and destroyers *Oriani* and *Ascari* were ordered to finish them off. The Battle of Pantelleria was another qualified Italian victory. Although three merchant ships subsequently reached Malta with 15,000 tons of cargo, the cost had been high. In return the only RM ship to suffer significant damage was *Vivaldi*.

The final phase

The failure of the RN to deliver adequate supplies to Malta in June meant another major effort was mounted in August. For the RN, this was a supreme effort with three carriers, two battleships, seven cruisers, and 24 destroyers escorting a large convoy of 14 merchant ships. Because of a crippling fuel shortage, the main Axis effort was made by submarines, aircraft, and torpedo boats as the convoy moved east from Gibraltar. However, enough fuel was gathered to enable an RM surface force of three heavy, three light cruisers, and 11 destroyers to sortie and deal the final blow against the convoy south of Pantelleria Island on the morning of June 13. Axis forces shredded the convoy – only five merchant ships reached Malta. But the RM cruiser–destroyer force was denied a chance to deliver the final blow when Mussolini recalled the force only hours from a potential interception.

After August, Axis fortunes in the Mediterranean waned. Axis ground forces in Egypt were decisively defeated in late October 1942 and Allied landings in French North Africa soon followed. The focus of the naval war shifted to the convoy routes to Tunisia as the Axis struggled to supply its

C

ORIANI AT THE BATTLE OF PANTELLERIA

At the Battle of Pantelleria on June 15, 1942, the RM committed a small force to stop the passage of the Operation *Harpoon* convoy to Malta. In a confusing daylight action, two Italian light cruisers, supported by five destroyers, attempted to get through the British escort to attack the convoy. On this day, the gunnery of the Italians was accurate. Although several British ships were damaged by gunfire, the Italian force was unable to attack the convoy directly. As the RM battled the convoy escort, Italian dive-bombers appeared and sank one merchant ship and damaged the tanker *Kentucky*, which was taken under tow. Another merchant ship was later damaged by air attack. The British commander decided to scuttle *Kentucky* and the other damaged merchant. The Italians came across the burning ships, and the *Oriani* and *Ascari* were ordered to finish them off. This scene shows *Oriani* shelling *Kentucky* from a distance of 13,000 yd. Later in the action *Oriani* torpedoed the tanker, but the torpedo that hit the ship failed to explode. The Battle of Pantelleria was one of the most successful actions by the RM's surface forces during the war.

Folgore photographed at Piraeus in August 1942. The view shows the aft 4.7in mount and depth charge rails on the stern. The funnel pointing up on the stern is part of the smoke generator. The ship was lost in a night encounter with British units a few months later. In this action, Folgore was able to fire all six of her torpedoes at close-range targets, but none hit. The destroyer was then taken under fire from light cruiser Argonaut and sunk by nine 5.25in shell hits that caused extensive fire and flooding. (M. Brescia Collection)

Several Soldati-class destroyers accompanied the RM's battle fleet when it left La Spezia and headed for Malta after the declaration of the armistice. On September 9, 1943, the fleet was attacked by 28 German Do-217 bombers carrying FX-1400 guided bombs. Battleship Roma was hit by two bombs and sank with heavy loss of life. Carabiniere rescued 112 survivors and headed for Port Mahon in the Balearic Islands where she, along with Mitragliere and Fuciliere, were interned. This photograph, taken in fall 1943, shows Carabiniere with Mitragliere moored inboard. The Italian ships were detained by the Spanish until January 15, 1945. (M. Brescia Collection)

last bridgehead. Allied airpower forced the RM's battle fleet to bases in northern Italy to avoid attack. This, and a lack of fuel oil, left the RM's destroyer force as the heaviest units available to defend convoys bound for Tunisia.

Allied airpower took the lead in convoy interdiction operations, but there were still clashes with Allied surface forces. On the night of December 2, an RM force of three destroyers and two torpedo boats escorted four merchant ships to Tunis. The convoy was attacked near Skerki Bank by three RN light cruisers and two destroyers. Again, the RM performed poorly in a night battle. All of the merchant ships were sunk and a light cruiser quickly dispatched destroyer *Folgore*. Before being sunk, the destroyer managed to fire all six of her torpedoes, but they missed. Destroyer *Da Recco* also managed to fire torpedoes at close range, but again with no success. She was taken under heavy fire and left dead in the water with 118 dead onboard. *Da Recco* was later towed back to port.

December convoys to Tunisia were hit hard by Allied interdiction. Of the 45 merchant ships sent on the "Route of Death," only 29 arrived. To augment this, Italian destroyers made 45 transport runs. Allied mining efforts were intensified; in January destroyer *Corsaro* was sunk and *Maestrale* damaged near Bizerte. Destroyer *Saetta* was mined on February 3, and *Malocello* and *Ascari* were lost to mines on March 24. By May, the supply route to Tunis had collapsed due to a lack of escorts and minesweepers.

The surrender of Axis forces in Tunisia in May 1943 brought the Mediterranean naval war to its final phase. The RM kept its battle fleet of two battleships, three light cruisers, and 11 destroyers in reserve with enough fuel for a final operation, but it was not employed when the Allies invaded Sicily in July or southern Italy in September. The new Italian government agreed to an armistice on September 8, 1943. All RM ships which could put to sea were ordered to Allied ports the following day. By this point, only 17 destroyers were operational with another six under repair. In the next

few days after the armistice, *Da Noli* was sunk by a mine and *Vivaldi* was hit by German aircraft off northern Sardinia and later foundered. *Sella* was torpedoed by German S-boats and sank. Two more ships were captured by the Germans and brought back into service. In total, 12 destroyers joined the Allies, although one was soon sunk in October 1943 by German aircraft. Of the six ships under repair, three were put into service by the Germans. The others were judged not worth the effort to return to service or were used for spare parts for the ships that were.

The Red Sea

Almost all RM destroyers operated in the Mediterranean, but it is little known that a force of seven destroyers began a war based in the Italian colony of Eritrea. This included the 5th Destroyer Flotilla of three Leone-class ships and the four ships of the Sauro class which comprised the 3rd Destroyer Flotilla. This small force was a major concern to the RN, since it was athwart a major shipping lane in the Red Sea, which ran to the southern terminus of the Suez Canal.

The ships deployed by the RM to the Red Sea were expendable, since there was no way they could be supplied or return to the Mediterranean once war broke out. This is why the RM chose to send seven of its oldest destroyers to the Red Sea. The operations of this small force were greatly restricted by shortages in fuel and spare parts. Once war broke out in June 1940, the destroyers were used to lay defensive minefields. The RM also used these ships to conduct six sweeps into the Red Sea between July and September to intercept British convoys, but no contact was made. The first contact with a British convoy was finally made on the night of October 20/21 by a force of four destroyers (*Pantera*, *Leone*, *Sauro*, and *Nullo*). These faced the escort of convoy BN7 which consisted of light cruiser *Leander*, destroyer *Kimberley*, and five smaller combatants. *Pantera* fired four torpedoes without success and retired with *Leone*. *Sauro* fired a couple of torpedoes at the convoy, but failed to score a hit. *Nullo* engaged *Leander* in a gun duel and was damaged. *Kimberley* finished off the destroyer with gunfire and a torpedo. *Pantera*, *Tigre*, and *Sauro* attacked convoy BN14 on the night of February 3, 1941. The British escort failed to damage the attackers, but no ships in the convoy were hit.

By March 1941, the fall of Massawa was imminent, so the Italians planned to use the remaining ships on a couple of audacious forays before they would have to be scuttled. The first mission was targeted against the port of Suez. This was abandoned when *Leone* ran aground on an uncharted rock on April 1, 1941 which forced her to be scuttled. After scuttling *Leone*, sister ships *Pantera* and *Tigre* returned to Massawa. The next day, a second mission, conducted by *Pantera*, *Tigre*, *Sauro*, *Manin*, and *Battisti* was targeted against Port Sudan, but this also went awry. The force was attacked by Swordfish bombers from RN aircraft carrier *Eagle*, which were based at Port Sudan. *Battisti* suffered engine problems and was scuttled by her crew off the coast of Saudi Arabia. *Sauro* and *Manin* were sunk the next morning by air attack northeast of Port Sudan. *Pantera* and *Tigre* proceeded to a point 15 miles south of Jedda on the coast of neutral Saudi Arabia and were scuttled by their crews. While the seven Italian destroyers deployed to the Red Sea inflicted no damage on the enemy, they did tie down British naval resources for the better part of a year.

RM DESTROYERS

Mirabello class

These were the RM's first large destroyers and the oldest destroyers still in service when Italy entered the war in June 1940. The three ships of the class were originally planned as 5,000-ton ships but, when completed, had a full load displacement of less than half that. Nevertheless, when they entered service these were capable ships with a very heavy armament combined with a high speed of 35kt.

Ship	Built at	Laid down	Launched	Commissioned	Fate
Carlo Mirabello	Ansaldo, Genoa	November 21, 1914	December 21, 1915	August 24, 1916	Sunk by mine April 30, 1941
Augusto Riboty	Ansaldo, Genoa	February 27, 1915	September 24, 1916	May 5, 1917	To USSR 1946; scrapped 1951

Armament

The main battery consisted of eight single 4in/45 gun mounts with a weak torpedo battery of two twin 17.7in mounts. Two 40mm single guns were fitted for antiaircraft protection. Between 1917 and 1918, a 6in/40 gun replaced the forward 4in mount, but this proved unsuccessful, since the lightly built ships were unable to take the stress of firing. The 6in gun was removed in 1919.

By the start of World War II, these ships were obsolescent, given their outdated gun and torpedo battery arrangements. They were employed in second-line duties during the war. *Mirabello* was lost without modification in 1941, but *Riboty* underwent several modifications to improve her antiaircraft and ASW capabilities. Two 4in/45 guns were removed in 1942 and another two the following year. Six 20mm/70 single antiaircraft guns were added and her depth charge capacity increased. In 1944, the torpedo tubes were removed. The ships were equipped to carry up to 100 mines.

Operational history

The third ship in the class, *Carlo Alberto Racchia*, was sunk by a mine off Odessa in the Black Sea on July 21, 1920. At the outbreak of World War II, the two remaining ships were based at Brindisi and operated in the southern Adriatic. After laying defensive minefields in the Gulf of Taranto in the first two months of the war, they shifted to escorting convoys to Italian forces in Albania. In October, they conducted shore bombardment of Greek targets after the Italian invasion of that country. Operating in this area, *Mirabello* struck a mine north of

Augusto Riboty photographed at Venice in November 1942 in a dark and light gray dazzle camouflage pattern. By this time, two of her original eight single 4in/45 mounts had been removed. The two ships of this class were obsolescent by the start of the war and were employed in secondary areas. *Riboty* survived the war to be scrapped in the 1950s. (M. Brescia Collection)

Cefalonia laid by RN minelayer *Abdiel* on April 30, 1941. *Riboty* continued on convoy escort duties in the Adriatic and Aegean Seas and on convoys to North Africa. The ship reached Malta to surrender when the armistice was declared. She was allocated to the USSR as war reparations, but the Russians rejected her due to her poor material condition. *Riboty* was scrapped in 1951.

Mirabello-class specifications	
Displacement	Standard 1,811 tons; full 2,302 tons
Dimensions	Length 340ft, 5in; beam 32ft; draft 10ft, 6in
Propulsion	4 boilers and 2 geared turbines generating 35,000 on 2 shafts; maximum speed 35kt
Range	2,840nm at 15kt
Crew	158

Leone class

The RM planned to build five more enlarged Mirabello class "light scouts." These ships were ordered before the end of World War I, but the general economic conditions during this period and the lack of steel meant that just three were started and construction only began in 1921. The class was named after the lead ship, *Leone* (Lion). The new ships were larger and heavier than the preceding class in order to accommodate the heavier main battery. The machinery fitted produced a top speed of 29kt. In the 1920s and 1930s, they were employed as flotilla leaders.

Ship	Built at	Laid down	Launched	Commissioned	Fate
Leone	Ansaldo, Genoa	December 23, 1921	October 1, 1923	July 1, 1924	Grounded April 1, 1941
Pantera	Ansaldo, Genoa	December 19, 1921	October 18, 1923	October 28, 1924	Scuttled April 3–4, 1941
Tigre	Ansaldo, Genoa	January 23, 1922	August 7, 1924	October 10, 1924	Scuttled April 3–4, 1941

Armament

The main battery consisted of eight 4.7/45 Canet-Schneider-Armstrong guns designed in 1918/19. Dual mounts were adopted, but their placement was not ideal. One mount was placed on the bow and stern, but the other two were placed amidships, which gave them a restricted arc of fire. The torpedo battery remained at two twin 17.7in mounts, later increased to 21in tubes. Two 40mm single guns and four 20mm single mounts were also fitted. The ships were equipped to carry up to 60 mines. It is unlikely that the ships were modified before being sent to Eritrea in 1939.

This excellent profile view of *Tigre* dates from February 1938. Designed as a light scout, the three ships in the class were heavily armed for their time, carrying four twin 4.7in mounts and two twin torpedo mounts. The placement of the main gun battery was not ideal, as can be seen here with one mount between the stacks and another mount aft between the two torpedo mounts. In 1938, the ships were reclassified by the RM as destroyers. (M. Brescia Collection)

Operational history

By 1940, these ships were obsolete. Their machinery was badly worn and their weapons dated. Assigned to the 5th Destroyer Flotilla, they fought a sporadic war with the RN between June 1940 and April 1941, as described above.

Leone-class specifications	
Displacement	Standard 1,743 tons; full 2,648 tons
Dimensions	Length 372ft; beam 34ft; draft 10ft, 2in
Propulsion	4 boilers and 2 geared turbines generating 42,000 on 2 shafts; maximum speed 29kt
Range	2,400nm at 16kt
Crew	206

Sella class

At the same time as the large scout destroyers were being constructed, the RM was building 1,200-ton destroyers. Two of these classes were not successful, so the RM ordered a new design from the Pattison yard in Naples for a larger design. These ships introduced several design features, which became standard in future Italian destroyer designs. The 4.7in gun was used for the first time on a destroyer and the standard size of the torpedo tubes was increased to 21in. Despite the class introducing several successful design features, these ships were plagued by unreliable machinery. Although the ships recorded 38kt on trials, by 1940 the ships' top speed was only 31kt under operational conditions. This was caused by worn machinery and greater displacement following modifications.

Overall, the class was not a success due to the machinery problems, limited endurance, marginal stability, and very low freeboard. Italian designers had tried to put too much on too small a hull.

Ship	Built at	Laid down	Launched	Commissioned	Fate
Francesco Crispi	Pattison, Naples	February 21, 1923	September 12, 1925	April 29, 1927	Captured in September 1943, returned to service as German *TA15*
Quintino Sella	Pattison, Naples	October 12, 1922	April 25, 1925	March 25, 1926	Lost September 11, 1943
Bettino Ricasoli	Pattison, Naples	January 11, 1923	January 29, 1926	December 11, 1926	Sold to Sweden in March 1940
Giovanni Nicotera	Pattison, Naples	May 6, 1925	June 24, 1926	January 8, 1927	Sold to Sweden in March 1940

This is *Sella* in 1939. The two ships in this class suffered from low freeboard, obvious in this view, and compromised stability, which is suggested by the large bridge and the two 4.7in mounts placed high up on the ship. To correct this problem, the second fire control director abaft the second stack was removed as was the searchlight at the base of the mainmast. This failed to correct the problem. The ships also suffered from unreliable machinery. *Sella* was sunk days after the armistice by two German S-boats. (M. Brescia Collection)

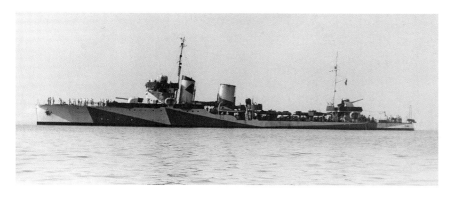

Armament

For the first time, an Italian destroyer (versus a larger "scout") was equipped with a 4.7in gun. When completed, the ships had a single 4.7in mount forward and a twin mount aft. In 1929, the single mount forward was replaced with a twin mount. The torpedo battery consisted of two twin 21in mounts. Light armament included two 40mm single guns and two 13.2mm machine guns. The ships could carry up to 32 mines.

Since the ships had stability issues, measures were taken to reduce top weight. A second gun director for the main battery, located abaft the second stack, was removed. The searchlight at the base of the mainmast was also taken off. The ship's boats abreast the forward stack were replaced by two 20mm single guns. Two more 20mm guns replaced the old 40mm mounts. Two depth-charge throwers were added to enhance ASW capabilities.

Operational history

Two of the ships were sold to Sweden in March 1940 because of Italy's desperate need for foreign exchange; they served in the Swedish Navy until 1947. At the start of the war, the remaining two ships, comprising the 4th Destroyer Flotilla, were based at Leros in the Dodecanese Islands. The destroyers operated in the Aegean on minelaying and escort duties. The highlight of these operations occurred in March 1941 when they transported the assault craft used to attack British shipping inside Suda Bay, Crete. These units sank a large tanker and damaged heavy cruiser *York*, resulting in her loss. When the British evacuated Greece in 1941, *Sella* was attacked by German dive-bombers by mistake and heavily damaged. At the time of the armistice, *Sella* was located in the northern Adriatic and was sunk by German S-boats *S54* and *S61*. *Crispi* was captured by the Germans at Piraeus and put into service as *TA15*. While in German service, she was sunk on March 8, 1944 by Allied air attack.

Sella-class specifications	
Displacement	Standard 970 tons; full 1,480 tons
Dimensions	Length 278ft, 6in; beam 28ft, 2in; draft 8ft, 10in
Propulsion	3 boilers and 2 geared turbines generating 36,000 on 2 shafts; maximum speed 35kt
Range	1,800nm at 14kt
Crew	253

Sauro class

This class was an improvement of the Sella-class units. It possessed the same basic configuration, but it was more heavily armed with two twin

4.7in mounts and substituted triple torpedo mounts for twin ones. Even though the ships were longer, heavier, and had a greater beam and freeboard, their seaworthiness was not improved. The ships were top-heavy, an issue exacerbated by the addition of a large fire control director atop the bridge in 1933. The ships recorded 37kt on trials, but their actual top speed under wartime conditions was only 30kt. Machinery reliability remained a problem.

This is a stern quarter view of *Francesco Nullo* in the late 1930s, a member of the four-ship Sauro class. One minor difference between the two classes was the second fire control director positioned aft between the torpedo mounts, as seen in this view. This was to allow the aft 4.7in mount to engage targets independently. It did not prove successful and was removed to save weight. (M. Brescia Collection)

Ship	Built at	Laid down	Launched	Commissioned	Fate
Cesare Battisti	Odero, Genova	February 9, 1924	December 11, 1926	April 13, 1927	Scuttled April 3, 1941
Daniele Manin	Cantieri Navali del Quarnaro, Fiume	October 9, 1924	June 15, 1925	March 1, 1927	Lost April 3, 1941
Francesco Nullo	Cantieri Navali del Quarnaro, Fiume	October 9, 1924	November 14, 1925	April 15, 1927	Lost October 21, 1940
Nazario Sauro	Odero, Genova	February 9, 1924	May 12, 1926	September 23, 1926	Lost April 3, 1941

Armament
These ships were more heavily armed than the preceding Sella class. The main battery consisted of two twin 4.7in mounts located in the same locations. The torpedo battery was increased to two triple 21in mounts. Light armament remained the same with two 40mm single guns and two 13.2mm machine guns. The ships could carry up to 52 mines. Since the ships were exiled to Eritrea and were sunk early in the war, they received no modifications.

Operational history
At the start of the war, the entire class was deployed to Massawa, where it formed the 3rd Destroyer Flotilla. The operations and fate of these ships has been related above.

Turbine shown entering Taranto in the late 1930s. The eight ships of the Turbine class were the last development of the Sella class; unfortunately for the RM, they suffered from the same stability and machinery problems. The layout of the Turbine class and the preceding Sauro class was virtually identical. *Turbine* had a busy wartime career. In 1942 she was moved into the Aegean and based at Piraeus, where she was captured by the Germans after the armistice. She was active for just over a year in German hands. (M. Brescia Collection)

Sauro-class specifications	
Displacement	Standard 1,058 tons; full 1,600 tons
Dimensions	Length 295ft, 10in; beam 30ft, 2in; draft 9ft, 6in
Propulsion	3 boilers and 2 geared turbines generating 36,000 on 2 shafts; maximum wartime speed 30kt
Range	2,600nm at 14kt
Crew	156

Turbine class
The eight ships of this class were the last in the evolution, which began with the Sella class. Four ships were funded in 1923 and four more the following year. In addition, four similar ships were built for the Turkish Navy. The configuration of the Turbine class was basically unchanged from the preceding two classes. The new ships were slightly longer and had a greater displacement, but

seaworthiness was not greatly improved. The ships also received a large fire control director atop the bridge, which only increased concerns with stability.

The design power of the machinery was increased to attain greater speeds, and on trials *Turbine* achieved 39.5kt. However, actual top speed under operational conditions was 31kt. The range of these ships was increased by additional bunkerage, but still remained limited.

Ship	Built at	Laid down	Launched	Commissioned	Fate
Aquilione	Odero, Genoa	May 18, 1925	August 3, 1927	December 3, 1927	Lost September 17, 1940
Borea	Ansaldo, Genoa	April 29, 1925	January 28, 1927	November 14, 1927	Lost September 17, 1940
Espero	Ansaldo, Genoa	April 29, 1925	August 31, 1927	April 30, 1928	Lost June 28, 1940
Euro	Cantieri del Tirreno, Riva Trigoso	January 24, 1925	July 7, 1927	December 22, 1927	Lost October 1, 1943
Nembo	Cantieri del Tirreno, Riva Trigoso	January 21, 1925	January 27,1927	October 14, 1927	Lost July 20, 1940
Ostro	Ansaldo, Genoa	April 29, 1925	January 28,1928	June 9,1928	Lost July 20, 1940
Turbine	Odero, Genoa	March 24,1925	April 24,1927	August 27, 1927	Captured September 1943; renamed German *TA14*
Zeffiro	Ansaldo, Genoa	April 29, 1925	May 27, 1927	May 15, 1928	Lost July 5, 1940

Armament

These ships were armed in the same manner as the preceding Sella class. The main battery consisted of two 4.7in twin mounts and the torpedo battery was comprised of two triple 21in mounts. Light armament remained the same with two 40mm single guns and two 13.2mm machine guns. The ships could carry up to 52 mines. Six of the ships were lost early in the war and thus received no modifications. The two that survived received slight enhancements to their antiaircraft battery. *Euro* and *Turbine* landed their old 1917 40mm guns and received four 20mm single mounts. *Turbine* subsequently received two single 37mm/54 mounts in place of one of her torpedo mounts.

Operational history

In June 1940, these ships comprised the 1st and 2nd Destroyer Flotillas based at Tobruk. This location meant that they were heavily engaged from the start of the war. Losses were therefore heavy, with six of the ships lost within months. The first RM destroyer sunk during the war was *Espero* on June 28, 1940 as mentioned above. Four sister ships were sunk in port by British aircraft. Swordfish torpedo bombers from *Eagle* sank *Zeffiro* in Tobruk harbor on July 5. *Euro* had her bow blown off, but was beached and later repaired. On July 20, the same aircraft torpedoed *Nembo* and *Ostro* in the Gulf of Bomba. Next to be lost was *Borea*, which was sunk by aircraft from carrier *Illustrious* in Benghazi. *Aquilone* was sunk by an air-dropped mine in the same attack. The two remaining ships continued active escorting convoys to and from North Africa. In 1941, *Euro* was escorting

Euro shown on March 12, 1942 on convoy escort duty in the southern Adriatic after modifications to reduce topside weight (note the absence of the second fire control director and that the stacks have been cut down) and the addition of more 20mm guns. *Euro* had an interesting wartime career, being badly damaged early in the war, escaping destruction at the hands of a British cruiser in November 1941, and then operating briefly with Allied forces after the armistice, before being sunk by German aircraft. (M. Brescia Collection)

NAVIGATORI-CLASS DESTROYER *DA VERAZZANO*

The 12 ships of the Navigatori class were the RM's largest and most heavily armed destroyers of World War II. This is *Da Verazzano* as she appeared in late 1940 before any wartime modifications. The ship retains her peacetime colors, but has had red and white stripes added on the forecastle to allow easier identification by Italian air force aircraft.

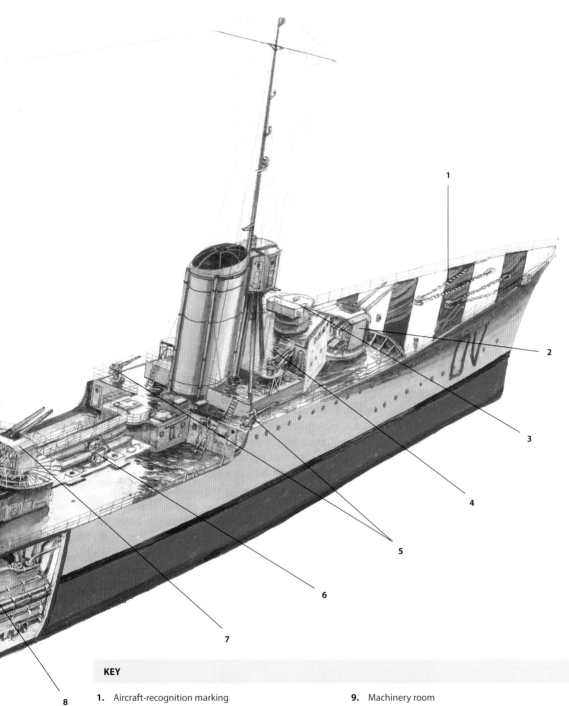

KEY

1. Aircraft-recognition marking
2. Forward twin 4.7in/50 gun mount
3. Fire control director for main battery
4. 13.2mm machine guns
5. 40mm single guns
6. Forward twin 21in torpedo mount
7. Amidships twin 4.7in/50 gun mount
8. Boiler room

9. Machinery room
10. 13.2mm machine guns
11. Rangefinder for main battery
12. Aft twin 21in torpedo mount
13. Searchlight
14. Aft twin 4.7in/50 gun mount
15. Mine paravanes

The start of the war ended the Navigatori modification program with *Da Recco* and *Usodimare* not receiving an overhaul. This is *Da Recco* off La Spezia in summer 1942 with her original straight stem. *Da Recco* was the only ship of the 12-unit Navigatori class to survive the war. (M. Brescia Collection)

During the war, it was obvious that the original light armament suite was insufficient for antiaircraft protection. Accordingly, by the end of 1941, seven 20mm/65 single mounts replaced the original fit. *Pancaldo* was fitted with another pair of 20mm/65 guns on her quarterdeck and *Da Recco* and *Pigafetta* received a pair of 20mm/70 guns on their quarterdeck. All of the guns placed aboard *Da Noli* were 20mm/70. Those ships surviving into 1942 had their aft torpedo mount replaced by two 37mm/54 antiaircraft guns. A few of the ships received radar, a rarity for an RM destroyer during the war. *Pancaldo* and *Da Recco* were fitted with the EC.3/ter and *Malocello* with a German Fu.Mo 21/39 De.Te device. These were all mounted above the bridge.

Operational history

These ships were considered important front-line units by the RM and had very busy wartime careers. Two of these ships, *Da Noli* and *Pigafetta*, conducted over 200 wartime sorties. For all ships, the predominant mission was convoy protection, but other missions included minelaying, fleet escort, and ASW sweeps. Later in the war they were also used as fast transports. Only one ship of the class survived the war.

Due to a major refit of the class under way, only nine ships were ready in June 1940. The class was assigned to the 14th, 15th, and 16th Destroyer Flotillas. Eight of the ships were present at the Battle of Calabria. After the battle, *Pancaldo* was caught in Augusta harbor by a British Swordfish and torpedoed. The ship was raised and repaired in July 1941 and reentered service in December 1941. In August 1940, *Vivaldi* sank British submarine *Oswald* by ramming. In October, *Da Noli* and *Tarigo* laid mines near Malta, which later sank two British destroyers. In 1941, convoy escort became paramount. *Tarigo* was the first of the class to be lost when she was sunk on April 16, 1941 by four British destroyers while on convoy escort duties. However, in this exchange torpedoes from *Tarigo* sank British destroyer *Mohawk*. The next month, *Pigafetta* and *Zeno* sank British submarine *Usk* off Sicily. Minelaying was a continuing mission; in June five Navigatori-class ships took part in laying a defensive field off Tripoli, which in December crippled Force K. The second ship lost was *Alvise Da Mosto* which was caught by a British cruiser 75nm northwest of Tripoli and sunk while trying to pick up survivors from a sunken tanker.

THE NAVIGATORI CLASS

1 The Navigatori class was among the RM's most successful destroyers. This is *Zeno* in October 1941 in an experimental "Claudus" disruptive camouflage. The ship presents an attractive appearance with its clipper bow (fitted in 1940), large bridge, two widely spaced stacks, and a heavy main armament of three twin 4.7in mounts and two twin torpedo mounts. Note the original 40mm and 13.2mm machine guns have been replaced by eight single 20mm/65 guns.

2 *Pessagno* shown with 86 P.200 mines in the late summer of 1941 in this view. Note the 86 P.200 mines placed on the minelaying rails on deck. The ship could carry up to 104 mines, depending on the type. The ship retains its 40mm and 13.2mm guns, which were soon removed and replaced by 20mm weapons, as well as the fire control director abaft the second stack.

3 This is *Pancaldo* in her early 1943 configuration. She was one of the most modified Navigatori-class ships. The modifications included the removal of the aft torpedo mount and the addition of two Breda 37mm/54 guns, the addition of the Italian-built EC.3/ter Gufo radar, and the fitting of ten 20mm/65 single guns, including an additional pair on the stern. *Pancaldo* was also one of the few RM destroyers to receive sonar.

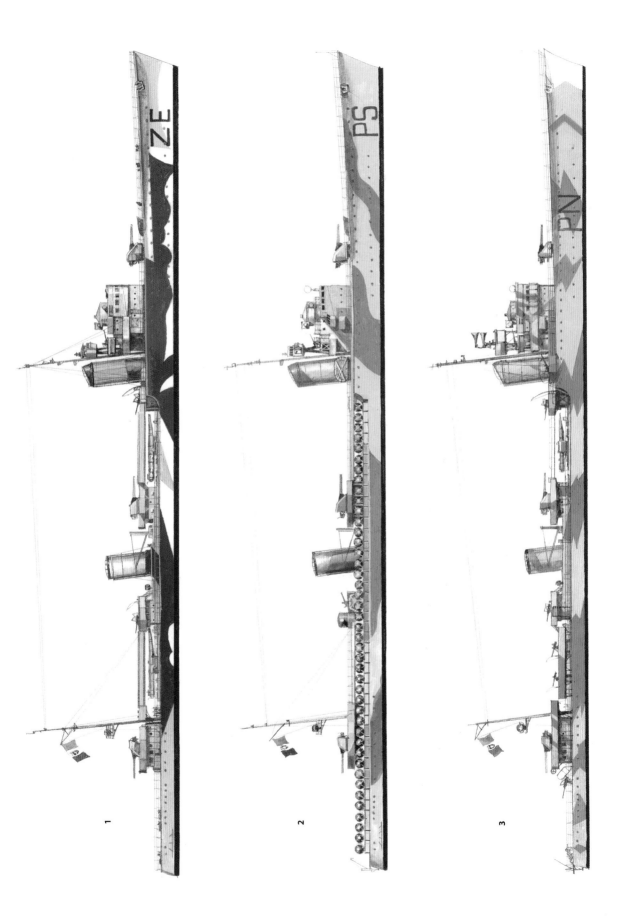

1

2

3

Convoy escort continued into 1942 with *Usodimare* contributing to the destruction of British submarine *P38* on February 25. The RN evened the score on May 29 when *Turbulent* torpedoed and sank *Pessagno* off Benghazi. *Usodimare* was mistakenly torpedoed and sunk by an Italian submarine in June and in October *Da Verazzano* was sunk by *Unbending* south of Lampedusa Island while on convoy escort duty.

In 1943, seven of the class were still in service. These were all eventually thrown into the effort to keep the Axis forces in Tunisia supplied. Two ships were lost in these operations: *Malocello* in March due to a mine and *Pancaldo* to USAAF air attack. When the armistice became effective, four more ships were lost. *Da Noli* and *Vivaldi* were both sunk during an attempt to attack German convoys between Sardinia and Corsica. *Zeno* was scuttled in La Spezia to avoid capture by the Germans. *Pigafetta* was captured in Fiume and entered service as *TA44*. She was sunk by air attack in Trieste in February 1945. Only *Da Recco* survived to operate with Allied forces. She remained in commission until July 1954 when she was scrapped.

Navigatori-class specifications (as of 1940)	
Displacement	Standard 2,125 tons; full 2,888 tons
Dimensions	Length 361ft (*Vivaldi* 352ft); beam 37ft; draft 15ft
Propulsion	4 boilers and 2 geared turbines generating 50,000 on two shafts; maximum speed 28kt (*Da Recco* and *Usodimare* 32–33kt)
Range	5,000nm at 18kt
Crew	230

Freccia class

Even as construction of the Navigatori class was under way, the RM resumed building smaller destroyers. These ships were slight improvements on the Turbine class, being slightly longer and heavier. The ships introduced a single-stack arrangement, which reduced topside clutter and gave better arcs of fire. Once again, soon after commissioning, the stability of this class was identified as an issue. Measures were taken to reduce top weight, which included the removal of the searchlight. The bilge keels were enlarged, and 90 tons of ballast added. This did not solve the issue, as was demonstrated by the fact that *Dardo* capsized on September 23, 1941 while undergoing an overhaul.

The ships recorded the usual high trial speeds – up to 39.4kt – but after the addition of more weight, wartime speeds were reduced to 30kt. The machinery arrangement did not employ the unit concept as used in the Navigatori class, and in service the machinery was found to be unreliable. Four similar ships were built in 1930 to 1932 for the Greek Navy.

Ship	Built at	Laid down	Launched	Commissioned	Fate
Dardo	Odero, Genoa	January 23, 1929	July 6, 1930	January 25, 1932	Captured; renamed German *TA31*
Freccia	Cantieri del Tirreno, Riva Trigoso	February 20, 1929	August 3, 1930	October 21, 1931	Lost August 8, 1943
Saetta	Cantieri del Tirreno, Riva Trigoso	May 27, 1929	January 17, 1932	May 10, 1932	Lost February 3, 1943
Strale	Odero, Genoa	February 20, 1929	March 26, 1931	February 6, 1932	Lost June 21, 1942

Armament

These ships were armed with the 4.7in/50 guns in a main battery consisting of two twin 4.7in twin mounts with one mount fore and aft. The torpedo battery consisted of two triple 21in mounts. As built, the light armament consisted of two 40mm single guns and two twin 13.2mm machine gun mounts. The ships could carry up to 54 mines.

Beginning in 1942, the antiaircraft battery was augmented. The original 40mm and 13.2mm guns were replaced by five or six 20mm/65 single mounts.

In 1943, the two surviving ships had their aft torpedo mount removed and replaced by two single 37mm/54 single guns. The aft fire control director was also removed and replaced by a twin 20mm/65 mount. Two more twin 20mm/65 mounts were added in the forecastle deck abreast the stack for a final total of 11 20mm guns.

The Freccia–Folgore-class ships suffered from poor stability. Dramatic proof of this was provided on September 23, 1941 when *Dardo* capsized at Palermo while she was shifting berths during an overhaul. The incident killed 40 men. (M. Brescia Collection)

Operational history

The 30kt top speed and unreliable machinery precluded this class from operating with the main battle fleet after 1940, when the faster battleships of the Vittorio Veneto class entered service. The four ships of this class comprised the 7th Destroyer Flotilla based in Taranto at the start of the war. Within days of the beginning of hostilities, *Strale* sank British submarine *Odin* off Taranto. These ships were present at the Battle of Calabria. After 1940, the class was almost exclusively used for convoy escort duties. The first ship, *Strale*, was not lost until June 21, 1942 when she ran aground near Cape Bon; the hulk was later destroyed by submarine-launched torpedoes. *Saetta* was lost to mines during convoy operations to Tunisia on February 3, 1943. *Freccia* was sunk in Genoa by an Allied air raid in August. The last ship, *Dardo*, was captured in Genoa after the armistice and was recommissioned in June 1944 as *TA31*. The ship served only a few months in German hands; she was damaged by air attack in October and written off.

The RM built eight ships of the Freccia and Folgore classes which entered service in 1931 and 1932. The only external difference between the two groups of ships was that the Folgore class was completed with stack caps, while the Freccia class had these added after commissioning. This view shows *Fulmine*, *Baleno*, *Lampo*, *Folgore* and *Freccia*, from left to right, at Messina in May 1935. The two ships built in Fiume, *Fulmine* and *Baleno*, had rounded fronts to their bridges, as seen here. All other ships had angled fronts. (M. Brescia Collection)

Freccia-class specifications (as of 1940)	
Displacement	Standard 1,520 tons; full 2,200 tons
Dimensions	Length 315ft, 5in; beam 32ft; draft 14ft
Propulsion	3 boilers and 2 geared turbines generating 44,000 on 2 shafts; maximum wartime speed 30kt
Range	4,600nm at 12kt
Crew	165

Folgore class

The four ships of this class were essentially the second quartet of the Freccia class. The main difference was a reduction of the beam to increase speed. This was unsuccessful, since the ships had the same stability problem, which required the same modifications already described for the Freccia class. The machinery exhibited the same reliability problems. Another difference was the much smaller endurance of these ships compared to the preceding class.

In February *Carabiniere* was torpedoed by British submarine *P36* south of Cape Spartivento. The destroyer survived and was towed to port, making her the only RM destroyer to survive torpedo damage. This is *Carabiniere* at Messina in March 1942 with a temporary bow. She proceeded to Leghorn under her own power where she was fitted with the bow of the uncompleted second-series Soldati-class ship *Carrista*. *Carabiniere* was converted into an ASW frigate and was not stricken until January 18, 1965. (M. Brescia Collection)

Armament

The Soldati class was built with a slightly larger amidships deckhouse in order to add an additional 4.7in/50 single gun. *Carabiniere* was the first to receive a 4.7in gun in this position, which replaced the 4.7in/15 illumination howitzer. In 1941/42, five more ships (*Ascari, Camicia Nera, Corazziere, Geniere,* and *Lanciere*) also received an additional 4.7in gun. All ships were initially fitted with two triple 21in torpedo mounts. The light armament consisted solely of 20mm/65 in eight single mounts. During the war, this was raised to 12–13 guns in single and twin mounts. *Fuciliere, Carabiniere, Granatiere,* and *Legionario* replaced their aft torpedo mount with two 37mm/54 single guns.

As the most modern RM destroyers, several ships received radar. *Carabiniere, Fuciliere,* and *Velite* were fitted with the EC.3/ter above the bridge in 1943. *Legionario* received the German Fu.Mo 21/39 De.Te in spring 1942.

Operational history

This class comprised the 8th, 11th, and 12th Destroyer Flotillas at the start of the war. They were assigned to the battle fleet and were a staple in all major fleet operations. All 12 ships were present at Calabria. In October 1940, the four ships of the 11th Destroyer Flotilla were engaged by British cruisers. *Artigliere* was badly damaged; under tow on October 12, she was caught and sunk by cruiser gunfire. Seven were present at Matapan, and all returned safely. Thereafter, the ships were drawn into convoy escort duties. In February 1942, *Carabiniere* was badly damaged by a British submarine, but was towed back to port. Following the Second Battle of Sirte, *Lanciere* foundered in heavy seas on March 23.

Losses mounted when the class was used to support convoy operations to Tunisia. *Aviere* was sunk by a British submarine off Bizerte on December 17, 1942. *Geniere* was sunk at Palermo on March 1, 1943 while in dry dock. In the same month, *Ascari* was mined and sunk in the Strait of Sicily. *Alpino* was struck by USAAF bombers in La Spezia on April 19 and sunk. Most of the remaining ships survived the armistice to surrender to the Allies. However, *Corazziere* was being repaired at Genoa and was scuttled on September 9 to avoid being captured by the Germans. *Fuciliere* and *Carabiniere* were

THE SOLDATI CLASS

1 This is *Alpino* as she appeared early in the war. The entire class began the war with two 4.7in twin mounts and two triple-tube torpedo mounts. The amidships position between the torpedo mounts was occupied by a 4.7in howitzer, which was later removed. The ship is in the standard early war light gray scheme.

2 Soldati-class ships were modified as the war developed. This view shows *Carabiniere* in 1943. Note the Italian-built EC.3/ter radar fitted above the bridge and the single 4.7in gun in the amidships position. The ship is in the standard dark gray camouflage scheme but with the Taranto curved-line variation.

3 The second-series Soldati-class ships were virtual repeats of the first series with minor external differences. Second-series ships had the amidships 4.7in/50 gun fitted upon completion (except for *Velite*) and 20mm guns. This is *Legionario* in late 1942, which also received the German-built Fu.Mo 21/39 De.Te radar. The ship is wearing the "parrot" scheme that added pea green and white to the usual light and dark gray pattern. The extra colors were later removed.

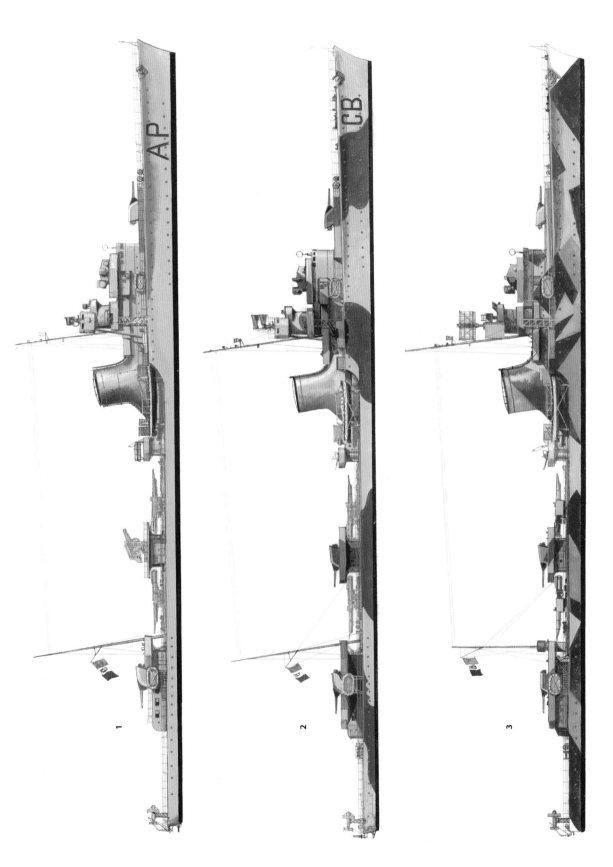

Only five of the seven second-series Soldati-class destroyers were completed. This is *Velite* soon after her commissioning, in early September 1942. Note the ship does not have the amidships 4.7in mount; instead twin 20mm/65 guns were fitted. These ships carried a maximum of 12–13 20mm guns for antiaircraft protection, which proved totally inadequate. (M. Brescia Collection)

temporarily interned in a Spanish port and reached Taranto in early 1945. *Artigliere* (the former *Camicia Nera* which was renamed on July 30 after Fascist-inspired names fell out of favor) and *Granatiere* reached Malta with the battle fleet in September 1943. Of the four remaining ships, *Artigliere* and *Fuciliere* were handed over to the USSR in 1949 and 1950, respectively. They remained in Soviet service until both were stricken in early 1960. *Carabiniere* had a postwar career with the Italian Navy as an ASW frigate and served until 1965. *Granatiere* remained active until 1958.

The second-series ships were commissioned beginning in February 1942 and were assigned to the 7th and 13th Destroyer Flotillas as part of the battle fleet. Two participated in the June 1942 Malta convoy battles and two in the August battles. *Velite* lost her stern to a British submarine attack in November 1942 and was repaired with the stern from the incomplete *Carrista*. *Corsaro* was mined off Bizerte in January 1943 and *Bombardiere* was sunk by British submarine attack off Trapani days later. The three surviving ships surrendered to the Allies and in 1948 were all given to France as war reparations. They saw no active service under the French flag and were stricken between 1951 and 1956.

Soldati-class specifications	
Displacement	Standard 1,830–1,850 tons; full 2,450–2,550 tons
Dimensions	Length 350ft; beam 33ft, 7in; draft 14ft, 1in
Propulsion	3 boilers and 2 geared turbines generating 50,000 on two shafts (2nd series 44,000shp); maximum wartime speed 34–35kt (2nd series 32–33kt)
Range	2,340nm at 14kt; 2nd series 2,500 at 14kt
Crew	215

Comandanti class

Design work began on the RM's last class of destroyer in 1941. The new design was based on the Soldati class, but was bigger, growing to almost 400ft in length with a 3,000-ton displacement. This allowed the fitting of a heavier main battery of four new 5.3in guns, laid out in two single mounts fore and aft in a superfiring arrangement. Antiaircraft protection was recognized as a weakness, so the new class was to be fitted with 12 37mm/54 single mounts. The ships retained two triple torpedo mounts placed abaft the large stack.

Aside from the heavier armament, the new class also had a new hull form, a redesigned bridge with radar mounted atop, and newly designed machinery capable of delivering 60,000shp and a top speed of 35kt. The RM planned to produce these ships in large numbers. Two series of eight ships were ordered in September 1941. A third series of another eight ships was later ordered, but in April 1943 the last four ships were canceled. Only two ships were laid down in Trieste in August 1943. Work was stopped weeks later after the armistice. Materials gathered at two other yards were abandoned at this time.

ANALYSIS AND CONCLUSION

As mentioned in the introduction, the performance of the RM's destroyers during the war was less than stellar. These ships were deficient in almost all regards. RM destroyers were designed for operations in the Mediterranean and thus possessed limited endurance. This lack of endurance translated into a short range of action, which precluded operations into the western or eastern Mediterranean. Most were lightly built and suffered from stability problems and poor seakeeping. In the Navigatori class for example, stability was especially bad after 50 percent of the fuel had been used. The system for replacing fuel with seawater was suspect and often resulted in contaminated fuel. Reducing top weight and adding ballast on the Navigatori eventually solved this problem, but the stability of other classes remained suspect. Not until the Maestrale class did Italian destroyer designers address this issue satisfactorily.

Italian destroyers did not compare well with their foreign counterparts. Despite an emphasis on a heavy main battery during the design stage, the firepower of RM destroyers was weak compared to foreign destroyers. Excessive dispersion experienced by the 4.7in main battery made accurate

OPPOSITE
These are builders' models of the never-completed Comandanti-class destroyers. Of the 20 projected units, only a handful were laid down and none were launched. The ships were similar in appearance to the Soldati class, as is apparent in this view. The top view depicts a ship of the first series with four 5.3in/45 single mounts and an antiaircraft battery of 12 single 37mm guns. The bottom view shows the planned second- and third-series ships with five 5.3in guns, a different antiaircraft battery of four quadruple 37mm mounts, and a modified bridge. Note both versions carry radar. (M. Brescia Collection)

ABOVE LEFT
The Royal Yugoslav Navy had four destroyers in service when Yugoslavia was attacked by Axis Forces in April 1941. The largest of these was the British-built *Dubrovnik*, commissioned in 1932. The ship was captured on April 17 and returned to service by the RM with the name *Premuda* and was heavily employed in convoy escort duties.

ABOVE RIGHT
The Italians also captured two of the three Beograd-class destroyers built for the Yugoslav Navy. These were almost 1,700 tons full displacement and mounted for four 4.7in gun and six torpedoes. This is *Sebenico* (ex-*Beograd*) pictured in spring 1943. *Ljubljana* was also captured and renamed *Lubiana* and served in the RM from November 1942 until she was lost off Tunisia on April 1, 1943. *Sebenico* was later captured by the Germans and served as *TA43* from October 1944 until the end of the war. (M. Brescia Collection)

gunnery all but impossible. During many clashes, British observers stated that Italian gunnery was accurate for range, but with the excessive dispersion, actual hits were very rare. On no occasion did an Italian destroyer sink an enemy warship by gunfire.

The ships also possessed a weak torpedo battery. While British ships carried eight to ten torpedo tubes, Italian destroyers carried only four to six, and during the war this was reduced to three on many ships. The resulting size of an Italian destroyer torpedo spread was small, and this was further reduced by the RM doctrine of holding some torpedoes in reserve. Only one enemy warship was sunk by an Italian destroyer torpedo during the entire war.

Most of the actions in which RM destroyers played a significant role were fought at night. This was a real problem, since the RM was not prepared to fight at night, while the British sought night engagements. Lack of night-fighting equipment and training, combined with the RM's total lack of radar until late in the war, meant that Italian destroyers were almost helpless at night.

Antiair warfare was also a salient weakness. This was not uncommon among other navies' pre-war destroyers, but the RM never addressed this problem and it became crippling after their destroyers were exposed to an increased air threat. RM destroyers lacked a dual-purpose main battery weapon, which meant that antiaircraft protection was almost entirely dependent on a small number of short-range 20mm guns. Invariably, when these ships were exposed to air attack, losses were heavy. ASW was another weakness, since RM destroyers did not possess the weapons, sensors, or training to conduct modern antisubmarine warfare.

These weaknesses translated into a dismal combat record. Of the 59 destroyers available at the start of the war in June 1940, combined with the five war-built ships, only 12 survived to join the Allies in September 1943. In return, RM destroyers sank only one British destroyer and a handful of submarines. The RM's destroyer force fought bravely, but its ships were ill-suited to modern war. The causes of the losses of Italian destroyers are outlined in the table below.

Fate of RM Destroyers						
Ships	Sunk by surface action	Sunk by submarine	Sunk by air attack	Sunk by mines	Scuttled or other causes	Surviving
Pre-war (59)	10	5	13	5	17	9
War-built (5)	0	1	0	1	0	3

BIBLIOGRAPHY

Bagnasco, Erminio and de Toro, Augusto, *The Littorio Class*, Naval Institute Press, Annapolis, MD (2011)

Bagnasco, Erminio and Brescia, Maurizio, *La Mimetizzazione Delle Navi Italiane 1940–1945 (Italian Navy Camouflage 1940–1945)*, Tuttostoria, Parma, Italy (2006)

Bragadin, Marc' Antonio, *The Italian Navy in World War II*, Naval Institute Press, Annapolis, MD (1957)

Brescia, Maurizio, *Cacciatorpediniere classe "NAVIGATORI"*, "Storia Militare Briefing" n. 9, Parma (2018)

Brescia, Maurizio, *Mussolini's Navy*, Naval Institute Press, Annapolis, MD (2012)

Campbell, John, *Naval Weapons of World War Two*, Naval Institute Press, Annapolis, MD (2002)

Fraccaroli, Aldo, *Italian Warships of World War II*, Ian Allan, London (1978)

Friedman, Norman, *Naval Anti-Aircraft Guns and Gunnery*, Naval Institute Press, Annapolis, MD (2013)

Friedman, Norman, *Naval Firepower*, Naval Institute Press, Annapolis, MD (2008)

Friedman, Norman, *Naval Radar*, Conway, London (1981)

Ghiglino, Marco, *Italian Naval Camouflage of World War II*, Seaforth Publishing, Barnsley (2018)

Greene, Jack and Massignani, Alessandro, *The Naval War in the Mediterranean 1940–1943*, Naval Institute Press, Annapolis, MD (2002)

Jordan, John, *Warships After Washington*, Naval Institute Press, Annapolis, MD (2011)

O'Hara, Vincent P., *Six Victories*, Naval Institute Press, Annapolis, MD (2019)

O'Hara, Vincent P., 'Italy: The Regia Marina' in *On Seas Contested: The Seven Great Navies of the Second World War*, Naval Institute Press, Annapolis, MD (2010)

O'Hara, Vincent P., *Struggle for the Middle Sea*, Naval Institute Press, Annapolis, MD (2009)

Sadkovich, James P., *The Italian Navy in World War II*, Greenwood Press, Westport, Connecticut (1994)

Whitley, M.J., *Destroyers of World War Two*, Naval Institute Press, Annapolis, MD (1988)

ABOVE LEFT
When the French Navy scuttled itself in Toulon in November 1942, the RM attempted to place several French destroyers back into service. Work proceeded on two Guépard-class large destroyers, but only *FR21* (ex-French *Lion*) was commissioned by the Italians. This is *FR21* at La Spezia in spring 1943. The forward torpedo mount has been removed but otherwise the ship retained her original appearance. The RM planned to use *FR21* and the other ex-French destroyers as fast troop-transports able to carry 400 troops. *FR21* was scuttled on September 9 and not returned to service by the Germans. (M. Brescia Collection)

ABOVE RIGHT
The Italians captured two more large French destroyers at Toulon and began work to return them to service. This is *FR22* (ex-French *Panthère*) moored in the Gulf of La Spezia in spring 1943, largely unmodified from her original appearance. Neither *FR22* nor *FR23* (ex-*Tigre*) served operationally for the RM. (M. Brescia Collection)

INDEX

Figures in **bold** refer to illustrations.